Acknowledgements

I would like to express my sincere and profound gratitude. Firstly to my parents, my mum and dad this would be impossible without their upbringing and relentless support. Special thanks go to the generals and servants of God who have assisted me in both nurturing the spiritual gifts I have and mentoring me. Special mention also goes to my spiritual parents **Apostle T and Pastor C Vutabwashe** words may not suffice the level of gratitude I have toward them. They came at a timely time, when I almost gave up on God they took me up in their shoulders as their own son and mentored me. Several sections of this book reflect their wisdom and tutoring as I don't have any wisdom of mine but what I have received. Apostle Vutabwashe you have pushed me to the edge, refused to give up until I have decided to do something to change this world. So much thanks go to the prayers of the saints of Heartfelt International Ministry.

40 Years In the Desert

When Trouble Runs You To Purpose

©2018

 @ncubethemzie

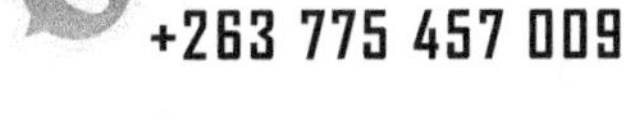 +263 775 457 009

ncubethemzie@gmail.com

 www.facebook.com/ncubethemzie

www.thembelanigrace.co.zw

Special tribute goes to the editorial team whose relentless efforts have yielded accurate syntax and grammar contained in this book. So much gratitude goes to you, the person reading this book, this book ceases to exist without you.

About the Author

Thembelani Ncube is a prolific writer an advocate for Christian liberty, ministration of the new covenant and the finished work of Christ at the cross.

His passion is to see the rise of an effective, different breed of young people "world shakers". People whose effect would be felt even generations way after them. He is a software developer by profession, a holder of a BSc (Hons) degree in Computer Science. His previous work is the grace masterpiece "Hope For A Sinner".

He has made wisdom his greatest quest, grace his greatest companion and revelation his mode of life. He stirs and tackles our everyday challenges, encourages the depressed, empowers the ordinary to do the extraordinary. His passion is to see the trodden walk in their predestined Godly purpose and gift.

40 years in the desert takes a leaf from the life of Moses whose roller coaster ride threaded into a halt as he fell from the gloss of Egypt to the dusk of the desert. It seeks to interpret the meaning of a divine call, what it means to be called of God. It places preparation as the essential ingredient for any endeavour in God. It's a dose of strength to the weary, a glow of hope to the disheartened and a seal of wisdom to the victorious.

Dedication

This book is dedicated to all the saints in Christ

Contents

Acknowledgements iii

About the Author vi

Dedication ix

Chapter 1: The Comfort Zone 1

Chapter 2: Identity Crisis 13

Chapter 3: The crown wearers..................... 43

Chapter 4: The most important Person........ 60

Chapter 5: His Voice and His manifestations 79

Chapter 6: Your problem is your solution 99

Chapter 7: Receiving the Art 118

Chapter 8: Welcome my King..........................133

Chapter 1

The Comfort Zone

So often at times we choose the comfortable option, the safe option. Have you ever done that? There's another option that says, I know God is bigger than this....

But when she could hide him no longer, she got a papyrus basket[a] for him and coated it with tar and pitch. Then she placed the child in it and put it among the reeds along the bank of the Nile. 4 His sister stood at a distance to see what would happen to him. Exodus 2:3 (NIV)

The cold breeze of the Nile swept across his soft body tissue leaving a pale image, cold water surged across his spine sending a chill down the bones. The basket suddenly became a cocoon of cold enveloped in darkness with rare rays of sunlight cast through the reeds. Just a day back he was embroiled in the comfort of the mother, the warmth of the hut, suddenly he found a new home amongst the croaking frogs and the beasts of the waters. It was a sudden turn of events and change of tales for the young Moses.

What was his first habitat became the first domain of rule when he struck his first plague [Exodus 7:17-18]. Did it register into the mind of a silent Moses that this was the beginning of a journey of the call of God in his life? A man predestined to be the saviour of the children of Israel was marred in uncertainty of life or death.

It came to pass that after the death of Pharaoh there arose another king amongst the Egyptians who knew not Joseph or his exploits. The population of the Israelites was increasing sharply hence it became a threat to the Egyptians, they resorted to the exercise of slavery and forced labour. Exodus 1 verse 14 says "They made their lives bitter with harsh labour in brick and mortar and with all kinds of work in the fields; in all their harsh labour the Egyptians worked them ruthlessly." As the political fabric unfolded in Egypt the king issued a decree to the midwives to kill all newly born sons to the Hebrews. The midwives feared the Lord so much and resultantly went against the order, the king resulted by issuing a nationwide directive saying **"Every son born of the Hebrews shall be cast into the river, every daughter will live"** [Exodus 1:22]

Amid political turmoil God's plan was in full swing, well-orchestrated as the pieces of setting his people free came to the fold. Our God is master of working in the chaotic. Environments of no hope are the most fertile grounds of God's handiwork and miracles. Genesis 1 :2 narrates "Now the earth was formless and empty, darkness was over the surface of the deep, and the Spirit of God was hovering over the waters." It is clear that the earth was in a shambolic state clearly without arrangement and empty but surprisingly this did not drive away the Spirit of God. Man, typically shun chaotic environments in favour of their comfort zones. In the following verses of Genesis chapter 1, it is well articulated how God through his Holy spirit created and formed this world. Man was created into a world that was a product of refactoring chaos, man's first lesson was supposed to be **"comfort is a result of chaos"**.

So often at times we choose the comfortable option, the safe option. Have you ever done that? There's another option that says, I know God is bigger than this, I know God has said that all things are possible to those who believe. I know God is a God of miracles. At times we find ourselves doubting with a strong but, a BUT that says this situation is probably bigger than God. Do you ever find yourself settling for second best? Do you ever find yourself choosing the easy option? What is it that stops you living and serving as God wants you to live? He has promised in whatever circumstance we find ourselves that He will never leave us or forsake us but we find ourselves fenced in by our own boundaries, we hide ourselves, we trap ourselves, we convince ourselves that we feel safe in our comfort zone and in our comfort zone, we can choose to ignore God, we can hide ourselves so deep we ignore His voice, or worse we get to the point where we believe that we are trapped in our comfort zone and that there is no escape from a prison we have created. Have you put walls around your comfort zone? Have you put a fence around the wall, so even if you try to escape your comfort zone there are additional barriers which prevent you from heading in the direction God is calling you to take? Has your comfort zone become a prison?

There's a story that I heard that says during the war a spy was captured and sentenced to death by a general in the Japanese Army. Before carrying out the sentence the general gave the spy a strange choice. He told him he could choose between a firing squad or a big black door. In a certain case the spy thought about the choice and chose the firing squad and within a few moments he was dead. The general turned to his assistant and said, "They always prefer the known way to the unknown." The assistant then asked the general, "What's behind the black door?" "Freedom!" Replied the general. "Behind the big black door is a passageway that leads outside, but only a few have been brave enough to see what was behind the door!"

What is the Big Black Door in your life? Is it the fear of the unknown that keeps us trapped inside our comfort zones! To be free from what has imprisoned us, we only need to open the door! Then we can get out of our comfort zone and step into the destiny that God has planned for us. We can be a part of the great adventure that God has planned for us. When we step out of our comfort zone, when we leave the prison we have created, when we leave behind the things that bind us and cage us - then we are in a place where we allow the Holy Spirit to fully work in us and through us.

Nehemiah's story, which is recorded for us in the Old Testament, is one of the great epochs of Christian history. Not only is

Nehemiah's story a manual on leadership, organization, and how to accomplish goals, it shows us what God can do through a man whose heart is totally and completely His. Nehemiah was a displaced Jew living a thousand miles from Jerusalem in what's known today as Persia, or Iran. He had risen to prominence as the cupbearer to the king of Persia, quite an honorary position that I believe made him live a comfortable life.

Yet one fateful day, some Jewish friends of Nehemiah returned from Jerusalem. And he asked them a question that ended up changing his life: "How is it with the people of Jerusalem?" And they said, "Nehemiah, it's not good. The walls are down, the gates are burned with fire, and the people are living in shame and disgrace." When Nehemiah heard this, it was like a shot to the solar plexus. It buckled him. It swept him off his feet and onto his knees! And he began to cry out to God… but not for just a moment. For four months he prayed until God showed him what to do! Let's go over that again **"not for a moment but for four months until God showed up"** [Nehemiah 1:1, Nehemiah 2:1]. I would think that what else would God have to wait for, he had a job to be done and a man willing to do it. Why this wait for four months. There is always preparation associated with every mission. Greatness can never be bought its only prepared for.

Nehemiah refused to ignore what God was doing in his heart which was to go back to Jerusalem to rebuild the wall. He could have continued to live in luxury in Persia, but Nehemiah's heart was a thousand miles away in Jerusalem. His heart was the heart of God. I believe God is doing exactly the same thing in the hearts of His people today. And that includes you! He's stirring your heart to do something for His glory. God is calling you to step out of your comfort zone, to do the unusual thing, to do the counter-cultural thing and to make His kingdom great!

Now, please, don't misunderstand me. You don't have to be a pastor, a missionary, or a super-spiritual star or hero! All you must do is have a heart for God and a willingness to get out of your comfort zone. It may be something as simple as just walking across the room at a party to talk to someone you normally would have ignored. Or inviting your neighbor over for tea. Or taking a co-worker to lunch to see how they're doing. Whatever it is, don't be afraid to step out of your comfort zone like Nehemiah did to do great things for God!

God is looking for men and women who have a heart for Him who want to take their lives to the next level. Men and women who want to step out of the maze of mediocrity and live for something bigger than themselves!

Chapter 2

Identity Crisis

There is nothing as perplexing as an identity crisis. When the environment perceives you differently than what you are really are.

Egypt in biblical times stands at the apex of civilization. It's a political powerhouse under the Pharaonic dynasty system. A hub of trade, central to finance and exchange of goods. Its economic lure is seen in the life of Joseph who eventually finds himself sold to Potiphar by the Medianites. Its intricate scenery and topography are punctuated by the pyramids an architectural masterpiece suggesting deep thrust engineering and scientific advancements. A political haven for Joseph, a safe habitat for Mary and Joseph and a refuge for Abraham and Sarah.

So Moses was educated in all the wisdom and culture of the Egyptians, and he was a man of power in words and deeds. Acts 7:22(AMP)

Exodus chapter 2:11 opens with Moses going to visit his fellow Hebrews matured in age probably in his thirties. Moses is brought up in the Egyptian palace as he had been adopted as the son of pharaoh's daughter. He is a prince and a symbol of royalty. He would be escorted by chariots of the Egyptian militia, he would command and be warranted service from his fellow countrymen as slaves. The Hebrew would bow, shiver in his presence. He was a symbol of authority and power. He learned arithmetic, geometry, and every branch of music, the hieroglyphics, the Assyrian language, and the Chaldean knowledge of the heavens. The presence of magicians and astrologers in Pharaohs court strongly quotes that he may have learnt astrology, practice of magic and interpretation of dreams. He had a great command of language and probably led great militant expeditions against the enemies of Egypt.

Possessing such attributes, he was greatly poised in frame to be the next Pharaoh.

Aside from his family all Israelites basically perceived Moses as evil as the rest of the Egyptian oppressors. Yet a few possibly knew of the keen battle that was rumbling within him, a battle of identity. At a point he may had to lash out a whip on the Israelites to act Egyptian silencing the deep anguish that echoed **"You are not Egyptian"**. Later, succumbing to the pain and guilt of oppressing your own blood. Imagine the thoughts that spiraled through his mother, brothers and sisters in face of such a scenery. The embarrassment that would engulf the mother who probably had been singing high praises of his "former son" to his fellows. This would shake and rumble the family foundation as a shadow of hesitance lingered through their minds **"Does Moses still remember us. Will he ever come back?"** Esther needed a reminder

of her identity to pursue the Jewish agenda what more of Moses who was raised in the comfort of the palace for years.

Moses could have been stuck in what may be termed an "identity Crisis". Having been adopted at the age of 3 months it is very much possible that Moses had forgotten about his origin which he honestly knew nothing about. This is what makes the life of Moses very intricate, what made him remember and act in support of his fellows.

He turned to look around, and seeing no one, he killed the Egyptian and hid him in the sand. Exodus 2:12 (AMP)

Another thought would suggest he probably heard some whispers in the corridors as he was growing up that he was adopted. This probably provided an inquisitive, unquenchable quest to probe into his identity. He would constantly secretly spy on the Israelite camp which places weight on the scripture "One day, after Moses had grown [into adulthood], it happened that he went to his countrymen and looked…." [Exodus 2:11]. There is nothing as perplexing as an identity crisis. **When the environment perceives you differently than what you are really are.**

I don't know of anything that is more crucial as a foundation to the Christian life, than for the believer to see what has been completed for him 'in Christ Jesus'. From Ephesians 2:7, we could say that this entire study is embraced within that wonderful phrase 'the riches of God's grace.'

So how do we define grace? A common definition is 'God's Riches At Christ's Expense'. Another definition is **'the unmerited favour of God'**. Both are true definitions, but the one that I like the best is simply **'God's love set free'**. You see grace incorporates all that God desired to do for mankind because of His love, which He is now free to perform, because His justice has been met through the sacrificial death of His son.

In most of Paul's letters there is a sharp distinction drawn between what **God has done for us by grace,** and **how we are to live in view of this fact.** The divine order that

God has established through these letters is to first sit and learn of your position in Christ, and then, in view of this position, the exhortation is given to live a life consistent with your position. In other words, the Christian life is becoming (in your experience) what you already are (in your position in Christ). This divine order is clearly seen in Ephesians, Colossians, and Romans amongst others. You should see a sharp distinction between the first three chapters and the last three Commenting on Ephesians, Watchman Nee said:

"Most Christians make the mistake of trying to walk in order to be able to sit, but that is a reversal of the true order. Our natural reason says, If we do not walk, how can we ever reach the goal? What can we attain without effort?

How can we get anywhere if we do not move? But Christianity is a queer business! If at the outset we try to do anything, we miss everything. For Christianity begins not with a big DO, but with a big DONE. Thus Ephesians opens with the statement that God has 'blessed us with every spiritual blessing in the heavenly places in Christ' and we are invited at the outset to sit down and enjoy what God has done for us; not to set out to try and attain it for ourselves."

Our endeavour is to set forth that which is DONE, and through faith, enable you to rest in the finished work of Christ and your exalted position in Him! The framework for the following has been taken from Lewis Sperry Chafer's book "Salvation." I recommend you read this book as it contains more than I could add here. Before looking at that which God has done for the believer in Christ, Chafer raises the following five points that are very important to remember.

1. These positions are not experienced, but are facts of the new life out of which precious experiences may grow. For example, justification is not experienced but the joy and peace that occurs because of this fact will be.

2. The Christian positions are not progressive. They do not grow or develop from a small beginning. They are as perfect and complete the instant they are possessed as they ever will be in the ages to come. For example, sonship does not grow, as an old man is

no more a son of his father at his death than he was at the day of his birth.

3. These positions are in no way related to human merit. They are made to stand on the unchanging Person and merit of the Son of God. The Christian is 'accepted (now and forever) in the beloved.'

4. Every position is eternal by its very nature. The consciousness and personal realization of these positions may vary with the daily walk of the believer, but the abiding facts of the new being are never subject to change in time or eternity.

5. These positions are known only through divine revelation. They defy human imagination, and since they are not experienced, their reality can be

entered into only by believing the Word of God. These eternal riches of grace are for the **lowliest sinner who will only believe.**

One more thought before you start racing through the list – Think! Yes, think about them. Meditate on them and what it means for you. You see, I've read lists like this before and I know the temptation to race through it. But I believe that these are truths that God would want to firmly establish within our hearts, for they glorify His character and show the extent of His work on the cross for us. So please, go slow, ask the Lord to reveal the truth in it, and meditate upon these things. Further on in his book *Sit, Walk, Stand*, Watchman Nee says:

"Our Christian life begins with the discovery of what God has provided. From this point onwards, Christian experience proceeds as it began, not on the basis of our own work but always on that of the finished work of another."

Every new spiritual experience begins with an acceptance by faith of what God has done – with a new 'sitting down' if you like.

Failure is almost a prerequisite for enjoying what God has done. God has hidden these truths from the proud and self-confident and as such they seldom seem interested, or care to believe that these things be of great benefit. But to those who truly see their need of God, the things of grace become the greatest delight! May you enter in new experiences of God's love as you accept by faith that which God has done 'in Christ.'

Before the world had even been created, God knew and chose those who would be saved, and in the course of time He called them to Himself. Do we fully understand it? No way! Not until He explains it all in heaven. Do we still believe it? Yes, both through the word of God and the experience of God's call upon our own lives. **In the eternal plan of God we are:**

Foreknown: Romans 8:29, "For whom He foreknew, He also predestined to become conformed to the image of His Son, that He might be the first-born among many brethren." (Also 1 Peter 1:2.)

Elect: 1 Thessalonians 1:4, "knowing, beloved brethren, your election by God." (Also, Romans 8:33, Colossians 3:12, Titus 1:1.)

Predestined: Ephesians 1:11, "In Him also we have obtained an inheritance, being predestined according to the purpose of Him who works all things according to the counsel of His will."

Chosen: 1 Peter 2:4, "Coming to Him as to a living stone, rejected indeed by men, but chosen by God and precious." (Also, Matthew 22:14.)

Called: Romans 9:11, ". . . that the purpose of God according to election might stand, not of works but of Him who calls." (Also 1 Thessalonians 5:24.)

How near to God has Jesus brought the believer? In our position, just as near as Christ is himself! – In our experience, just as near as we wish to go! His blood has been poured out for the sins of the world and the temple curtain has been torn in two!

Reconciled: By God: 2 Corinthians 5:18, "Now all things are of God, who has reconciled us to Himself through Jesus Christ." (Also, Colossians 1:20.)

To God: Romans 5:10, ". . . when we were enemies we were reconciled to God through the death of His Son." (Also 2 Corinthians 5:20.)

Redeemed: Colossians 1:14, "we have redemption through His blood, the forgiveness of sins." (Also 1 Peter 1:18, Romans 3:24.)

Brought Near: Ephesians 2:13, "But now in Christ Jesus you who once were far off have been brought near by the blood of Christ."

Given Access: Ephesians 2:18, "For through Him we both have access by one Spirit to the Father." (Also, Ephesians 3:12, Romans 5:2, Hebrews 4:14-16, 10:19- 20.)

Can someone be born, then become unborn? Can a son in a family somehow cease from being a son? Or can someone who has been adopted, be un-adopted? No, no, and finally, no! If you have been born into a family then you may change your name, but you cannot change your D.N.A and you are forever a son of your father. The same applies for our spiritual birth! The believer is a son of God Himself, born again of incorruptible seed and because of this we cry 'Abba Father!' – literally 'daddy'.

Born again: 1 Peter 1:23, ". . . having been born again, not of corruptible seed but incorruptible." (Also, John 1:12, 3:7.)

Sons of God: 1 John 3:2, "Beloved, now we are sons of God." (Also 2 Corinthians 6:18, Galatians 3:26.)

New Creation: 2 Corinthians 5:17, "Therefore, if anyone is in Christ, he is a new creation." (Also, Galatians 6:15, Ephesians 2:10.)

Adopted: Romans 8:15, "you received the Spirit of adoption by whom we cry out, 'Abba, Father.'" (Also, Galatians 4:5.)

Heirs: Galatians 4:7, "Therefore you are no longer a slave but a son, and if a son, then an heir of God through Christ."

A good question is 'Do you have to be perfect to go to Heaven?' Most say no, as no one is perfect. Yet could a perfectly holy God allow anything less than perfection into

His presence? Obviously not! The answer is therefore yes, you do have to be perfect, but how could this ever be achieved by a sinful creation? In Christ, righteousness and perfection is a gift! His declaration is that believers are forever justified – a position that not only means 'just as if I had never sinned', but also, 'just as if I had done everything right!' Wow!

Justified: Romans 5:1, "Therefore, having been justified by faith, we have peace with God." (Also, Romans 3:24, 8:30, 1 Corinthians 6:11, Titus 3:7.)

Righteous: Philippians 3:8,9, ". . . that I may gain Christ and be found in him, not having a righteousness of my own that comes from the law, but that which is through faith in Christ." (Also, Romans

3:22, 5:17, 10:3-4, 1 Corinthians 1:30, 2 Corinthians 5:21.)

Sanctified: 1 Corinthians 1:30, "Christ Jesus, who became for us... sanctification." (Also 1 Corinthians 6:11, Hebrews 10:10.)

Made Perfect: Hebrews 10:14, "by one sacrifice he has made perfect forever those who are being made holy." (Also see Hebrews 10:1-2 for the results of being 'made perfect'.)

Accepted: Ephesians 1:6, "to the praise of the glory of His grace, by which He has made us accepted in the Beloved." (Also 1 Peter 2:5.)

Forgiven: Colossians 2:13, "God made you alive with Christ. He forgave us all our sins."

(Also, Colossians 1:14, 3:13, Ephesians 1:7, 4:32.)

Complete: Colossians 2:10, "And you are complete in Him.'"

In a parable about the kingdom of God [Matthew 13:44], Jesus likened Himself to a man who found a treasure in a field. And because of His immense joy, He sold all that he had so that he could purchase that field. The treasure within the field stands for those in the world who believe in His name. For them, He was willing to give up all that He had (His life) and 'for the joy set before Him, He endured the cross!' We are the Fathers gift to the Son, His bride, His inheritance and His joy! Amazing.

His Gift: John 6:37, "All that the Father gives Me, will come to Me, and the one who comes to Me, I will certainly not cast out." (Also 10:29, 17:6,11,12,20)

His Bride: 2 Corinthians 11:2, "I promised you to one husband, to Christ." (Also, Ephesians 5:25-32, Revelation 19:7, John 3:29.)

His Inheritance: Ephesians 1:18, "that you may know the hope to which he has called you, the riches of his glorious inheritance in the saints."

His Possession: Ephesians 1:14, ". . . who is a deposit guaranteeing our inheritance until the redemption of those who are God's possession."

Each believer is also given the Holy Spirit, not only as our means of living the Christian life in this age, but also as a guarantee that as God's possession we will participate in the glory of the age to come! There is no true Christian alive that has not been given the Holy Spirit.

Born: John 3:6, "Flesh gives birth to flesh, but the Spirit gives birth to spirit."

Baptized: 1 Corinthians 12:13, "For by one Spirit we are all baptized into one body."

Indwelt: 1 Corinthians 6:19, "Do you not know that your body is a temple of the Holy Spirit, who is in you?" (Also 2:12, John 7:39, Romans 5:5, 8:9, 2 Corinthians 1:21, Galatians 4:6.)

Sealed: Ephesians 1:13-14, "having believed, you were sealed with the Holy Spirit of promise, who is the guarantee of our inheritance."

Think of it – when we were sinners and enemies of God, He fully justified us from every charge because our faith in the work of His precious son Jesus. How much more now, as His treasured possession, will believers find themselves the object of His care!

Objects of His Love: Ephesians 2:4, "But God, who is rich in mercy, because of His great love with which He loved us..." (Also 5:2, 1 John 3:1.)

Objects of His Grace: Romans 5:2, "through whom we have gained access by faith into this grace in which we now stand." (Also, Ephesians 2:7,8 Titus 2:12,13.)

Objects of His Power: Ephesians 1:19, "and his incomparably great power for us who believe." (Also, Philippians 2:13, 1 Peter 1:5.)

Objects of His Faithfulness: Hebrews 13:5, "For He has said 'I will never leave you or forsake you." (Also, Philippians 1:6, 1 Corinthians 1:8-9, Jude 24.)

Objects of His Peace: Philippians 4:9, "the God of peace will be with you." (Also 4:7.)

Objects of His Encouragement: 1 Thessalonians 2:16, "by his grace gave us eternal encouragement and good hope." (Also, Romans 15:4-5.)

Objects if His Intercession: Hebrews 7:25, "Therefore he is able to save completely those who come to God through him, because he always lives to intercede for them." (Also, Romans 8:34, Hebrews 9:24.)

Last, but most important of all, He has given us a heavenly citizenship – where we will be fellow heirs with the King of Kings! We live as strangers and exiles on this earth, far from our true home to come. We are ambassadors of God in a country not our own. But our heavenly home is assured, and our inheritance is waiting, kept safe by God himself!

Heavenly Citizens: Philippians 3:20, "For our citizenship is in heaven." (Also, Ephesians 2:19, Hebrews 12:22.)

God's Household: Ephesians 2:19, "... but fellow citizens with God's people and members of God's household." (Also 3:15, Galatians 6:10.)

Heavenly Inheritance: 1 Pet 1:4-5, "... and into an inheritance that can never perish, spoil or fade—kept in heaven for you, who through faith are shielded by God's power." (Also, Ephesians 1:14, Colossians 3:24, Hebrews 9:15.)

From the simplicity of a flower to the complexity of space, the more mankind explores the work of God. The more we stand in awe of its perfection. We can now examine the properties of God's creation right down into the cellular level, and this only confirms the thought that God has intelligently created everything, and His work is perfect and complete. With such a creative and all-powerful God, do you think He would complete anything less than perfection in His most important work – our salvation? The riches of His grace detailed above are just part of the fact that confirm that He has indeed completed His most perfect work in those that believe! The new creation is the most wondrous of all His creations!

Ok, so there is still one more thought...but it is something awesome to consider. Commenting on the entire list of the work done for the believer, Lewis Sperry Chafer wrote the following:

These marvels of grace constitute that 'good work' which He has but begun in those who trust Him. To this much more is yet to be added according to Phil 1.6 "He that began a good work in you will carry it on until the day of Christ Jesus." The 'riches of grace' are the beginning; the final presentation in glory in the likeness of Christ will be the completion. Such a final perfection and such an eternal being is the greatest divine undertaking for the one who has been lost in sin. Nothing less than this would satisfy His boundless love.

The "riches of God's grace," that is, His love set free, is incredible! I hope you have seen something more of His amazing work for everyone who has been born again. But like Chafer says, it's only the beginning! One day, when He comes again, the process shall be complete, and we shall be changed into His very likeness. And then, for the ages that are to come, His bride shall be a visible witness to the incredible kindness and grace of God. (Ephesians 2:7) Let me end with a quote which seems appropriate and will one day be reality...

"Grace is but Glory begun, and Glory is but Grace perfected." — Jonathan Edwards

Chapter 3

The crown wearers

After Moses killed the Egyptian he came to the climax of interpersonal conflict, an "identity crisis." He became too Egyptian to be Israelite and too Israelite to be Egyptian. Moses starred in his own version of "How to Get away with murder"

For Christ sent me not to baptize, but to preach the gospel: not with wisdom of words, lest the cross of Christ should be made of none effect. 1 Corinthians 1:17 (KJV)

Paul renounces the "wisdom of words." He says that he was sent to "preach the gospel, not with wisdom of words, lest the **cross of Christ should be made of no effect.**" It is very clear, therefore, that there is an excellence, elegance and eloquence of language which would deprive the gospel of its due effect. I have never yet heard that the cross of Christ was made of no effect by great plainness of speech, nor even by ruggedness of language—but it is the "wisdom of words" which is said to have this destroying power. Oh, dreadful wisdom of words! God grant that we may be delivered from making attempts at it, for we ought earnestly to shun anything and everything which can be as mischievous in its influence as to make the cross of Christ of no effect. The "wisdom of words" works evil at times by veiling the truths of God which ought to be set forth in the clearest possible manner.

The essence of the preaching of the cross, is objectionable to many minds and, therefore, certain preachers take care not to state it too plainly. Prudently, as they call it—craftily, as the Apostle Paul would call it—they tone down the objectionable features of the great sacrifice, hoping by pretty phrases to somewhat remove the "offence of the cross."

At the pinnacle of his call, Elijah persecuted three-hundred prophets of Baal [1 Kings 18], yet in the next chapter he escaped from a single woman called Jezebel [1 Kings 19].

How is it possible that a man who healed by casting his shadow goes before God to ask for the removal of a thorn in his flesh [2 Corinthians 12:9]. **How is it possible** that Jesus, as powerful and anointed as He was, picks as a disciple a man who was going to betray Him? How again Stephen, whilst preaching the gospel during the early church era when the gospel needed to take flight to other parts of the world, was killed for its sake [Acts 7:54-59].

We are living at a time where the message of the cross has been distorted within the church. It seems old fashioned to still speak of the relevance of "dying to the cross". I need to reach the actual you, after all the lights and buzz are gone, after all the hype and celebrity status has been cast away. After all the pretense is taken away, after the make-up, what remains is the genuine you. That person who accepts that even despite all the messages you have heard about the gospel at some point you still struggle. You have prayed about it, fasted about it, and yet still there is that nagging problem that seems not to go away. It may seem like people don't celebrate you or maybe your partner seems comfortable with everybody else except you or no matter how much you try it seems no one accepts you as you are. I may not exhaust all the paradigms, but everyone has a peculiar problem. Paul faces a similar dilemma and he goes back to God three times seeking for the removal of the thorn that was in his flesh. The fact that we're not primed of what was the thorn in his flesh means it was an **embarrassing, unpleasant**

sight for a man of the pedigree of Paul. He is the man who wrote more than two thirds of the new Testament. This is the man who goes to the Corinthian church which is peculiar of being competent in all the spiritual gifts and says, **"I speak in tongues more than all of you."** Despite his immense exploits the response of God in wake of his trouble was **"My grace is sufficient for you. My strength is made perfect in your weaknesses."** Well sometimes there seems to be some problems that God does not take away instantly. If we have prayed about it, it can only mean one thing, it's there to achieve something to the will of God. There are some problems that have nothing to do with the devil, they are sent by God himself to fix us, to align us to His will. What were the thoughts that swirled around the mind of Joseph the dreamer as he lay in a dark pit at the wake of abandonment by his brothers? He succumbed to the pain of being betrayed by his own blood. The heartache that echoed and re-echoed through our Lord Jesus Christ as the massive throng shouted, "Crucify Him," yet it's the same crowd that He fed, healed and ministered the word to. In all these circumstances God was part of it. He used circumstances to channel His will.

God writes a letter of invitation to His church. In Matthew 16:24, we have this famous verse on discipleship based on the lesson from Jesus' sacrifice. Jesus earned the crown as the King of kings and Lord of lords and will reign supremely on this earth because of first suffering on the cross. His position of exaltation is because of His obedience and humility unto the cross. He accomplished the Father's will by going to the cross of Calvary.

Then he said to them all: *"**Whoever wants to be my disciple must deny themselves and take up their cross daily and follow me.** Matthew 16 v24 (NIV)*

I wonder how many of us know very much about cross bearing, including me. We just don't relish sacrifice for Him. In the context, Peter wasn't willing for Christ to suffer, and probably was not wanting to suffer himself. I believe the two most likely go together. **If we don't put much emphasis on the death of Jesus Christ, we might be demonstrating our unwillingness to suffer for the Savior.**

Verse 24 makes it clear that God wants us to be people of impact— who are dangerous for Christ. He asks us to do three things. First, we are to deny ourselves. This doesn't mean giving up coffee or cinnamon rolls or whatever is your favorite treat. It doesn't mean giving up a specific thing. It means giving up everything. It means saying "no" to self and submitting to God— whatever He asks. How do I know if I am willing to do the will of God? **If we are willing to say "no" to God, we are not willing to do His will.**

Second, Jesus asks us to take up our cross. The cross is an instrument of death— death to my will. I must die to self. The condition of discipleship begins with dying. There are no crown wearers in heaven unless there is cross bearing on earth. The cross is something you take up or lay down voluntarily. For Christ the cross was a symbol of submitting completely to the Father's will. He took it up voluntarily. It is the same for us. When we take up our cross, we take up His will not our own.

Third, Christ calls on us to follow Him. Where He leads I will follow. Deep down inside some of us say we are willing to go anywhere, except Africa or Indonesia or across the street. If we are serious about the Christian life, we are willing to follow Him wherever He leads. If we don't live our lives that way, we waste it, **because there are no crown wearers in heaven who were not cross bearers on earth.**

Christ comes from Pilate's hall with cumbersome wood resting on his shoulders, but through weariness he travels slowly. His enemies half-afraid of his emaciated appearance that he may die before reaching the place of execution, allow another to carry his burden. The tender mercies of the wicked are cruel; they cannot spare Him the agonies of dying on the cross, but they will therefore remit the labour of carrying it.

***They forced into service a passer-by coming in from the countryside, Simon of Cyrene (the father of Alexander and Rufus), to carry His cross.* Mark 15:21 (AMP)**

No one died with Christ on the cross, yet another person did carry the cross for Him. This world was redeemed by a price and that is Christ alone. The ransom was paid by Christ; that was redemption by price, but power is wanted to dash down those idols, to overcome the hosts of error. Where is it to be found? In the Lord of hosts who shows His power in the in the sufferings of Christ and of His Church. The church may have to suffer, that the gospel may be spread by her means. This is what the apostle meant when he said:

Now I rejoice in my sufferings on your behalf. And with my own body I supplement whatever is lacking [on our part] of Christ's afflictions, on behalf of His body, which is the church. Colossians 1:24 (AMP)

There was nothing behind in the **price,** but there is something behind in the manifested power. We must continue to fill up the measure of the revealed power, carrying the cross with Christ. It is of paramount

importance to note that Jesus does not suffer to exclude your suffering. He bears the cross, not that you may escape it but that you may also be able to endure it. Christ does exempt you from sin but not from suffering. He does take the curse of the cross, but He does not take the cross of the curse away from you. Remember careful that and expect not to be excluded from suffering.

In our case and so was Simon's, **it's not our cross but Christ's cross** that we carry. When you are treated badly for your godliness, when your religion brings the trial of cruel mocking upon you, remember that it is not your cross, it is Christ's cross. Do not forget that you bear the cross in partnership. It is the opinion of some commentators that

Simon carried only one end of the cross not the whole of it. That is very much possible. Christ may have carried the heavier end, against the traverse beam and Simon bore the lighter part. Others believe he carried the whole lot. Either way he carried the wood part of it. He did not bear **the sin that made it such a hefty load.** Christ transferred to Simon the outward frame i.e. the wood, but the curse of the tree which is our sin and its punishment rested of Jesus' shoulders still. Dear friend in all your sorrow there is not even a drop of wrath. Jesus took the wrath and Jesus took the punishment of your sins. Now all that you endure is but for His sake, that you may be conformed to His image and aid in gathering His people to His family.

Although Simon carried Christ's cross, he did not volunteer to do it, but he was compelled to do so. Beloved, I fear that most of us, if we ever do carry it, carry it by compulsion. At least when it first comes onto our shoulders, we do not like it and would run from it, but the world compels us to bear Christ's cross. Cheerfully accept this burden dear servants of the Lord.

Simon, although he had to carry the cross of Christ for a short while, it gave him lasting honour. The *Via Dolorosa*, the Latin term for the path that Jesus followed to the Mount of Doom could have been a couple of yards or so. Irrespective of the distance that Simon carried the cross his name is in the Holy book forever. A few times the sun will go up and down the hill, a few more moons will wax and wane and then we shall receive the glory:

*For our **light affliction,** which is **but for a moment,** worketh for us a far more exceeding and eternal **weight of glory;***

2 Corinthians 4:17 (KJV)

After Moses killed the Egyptian he came to the climax of interpersonal conflict, an "identity crisis." **He became too Egyptian to be Israelite and too Israelite to be Egyptian.**

His outward appearance portrayed an Egyptian identity, while the killing act portrayed a contrary Israelite one. He left the palace and fled to the desert. A hostile climatic environment, scorching heat, sand storms became the sight of his day. The time had come for the almost "next Pharaoh" to align to God's will, to carry the cross. There is no affliction which is favorable or rather enjoyable. However, we can comfort ourselves with this thought: that it will all work unto the eternal weight of glory. Before it takes flight, every call needs time of preparation, and Moses is taken to a solitary place in the desert.

Chapter 4

The most important Person

He is not a thing. He is not the wind. He is not an earthquake. He is not a dove. He is a person and he is the most important person on earth. Do you know Him?

When Pharaoh heard about this matter, he tried to kill Moses. Then Moses fled from Pharaoh's presence and took refuge in the land of Midian, where he sat down by a well.
Exodus 2:15 (AMP)

As the rumors took flight of what the prince Moses had done, they made their way into the avenues of Pharaoh's ears. Catapult by anger, he sought the life of the "good-boy-gone-bad." I can only imagine what his thoughts were; Moses having been raised in the Egyptian courts from a tender age and these were his repayment terms, **really!** In pure financial terms he was a sink investment, or rather a bad return of investment. He took flight and dashed into the desert [Midian] with Egyptian armies hot on his heels. The bible says, "he sat down by the well." A plethora of thoughts must have flooded his mind: "I'm a murderer; for what benefit did I do that? I have lost my royalty status," with comforting ones like "I did it for my fellow brothers."

It was in the desert where Hagar's tears plummeted down the cheeks and cascaded from the chin after being sent away by the father of her son. Abraham sent them away at Sarah's request. Her ability to conceive had brought her to trouble. A gift to conceive that other women like Rebekah and Hannah at some point sought with tears had brought Hagar to her knees. It seemed as if she was at fault, when it was the same Sarah who offered her to Abraham. Afflicted with contempt and anger, her lady now sought for them to be cast into the desert.

Having reached a place of desperation, where the water and bread had run out, she decided to abandon the young Ishmael. However, at that point of despair and confusion the Lord intervened:

God heard the voice of the boy [Ishmael], and the angel of God called to Hagar from heaven and said to her, "What troubles you, Hagar? Do not be afraid, for God has heard the voice of the boy from where he is [resting]. ¹⁸ Get up, help the boy up, and hold him by the hand, for I will make him a great nation." Genesis 21:17-18 (AMP)

In what started as an eviction, Ishmael culminated to an ingredient to build a great nation. Elijah fled into the desert at the pursuit of Jezebel. As he sat under the broom bush, he prayed that he might die.

But he himself went a day's journey into the wilderness, and came and sat down under a juniper tree: and he requested for himself that he might die; and said, it is enough; now, O LORD, take away my life; for I am not better than my fathers. 1 Kings 19:4 (KJV)

After being baptized by John in the River Jordan, Jesus was led by the **Holy Spirit** into the wilderness (desert). Now let's pay attention to an important detail, *He was led by the Holy Spirit into the desert*. Before you yell at the devil and send him those ballistic missile tongues, take your make-up off and get yourself to understand that God himself can send you to the desert. The only way we can withstand any affliction or desert condition is only through the guidance and strengthening of the Holy Spirit. This leads us to the most important person in my life, the Holy Spirit.

There is common understanding in the body of Christ of the presence of the God head. The God head is God the father, the Son and the Holy Spirit. Perhaps is your understanding you have head of the term "trinity". I would rather not use that term as it does not exist in the bible in preference to the term "God head," as it dispels a major misconception that the Holy Spirit is the least of the God head. The proposed hierarchy is that God the Father is first, the Son second and the Holy Spirit last, and such an understanding has plunged the church into its current demise.

There seems to be no apparent explanation of the difference of the church in the days of Acts and now. However, the answer is very clear and it's simply that we are ignoring the Holy Spirit. God the Father, the Son, and the Holy Spirit are all equal in majesty and power. There are basically two questions to answer in the study of the Holy Spirit: Who is the Holy Spirit? And Why the Holy Spirit?

In the New Testament, Paul says that "God is one" [Galatians 3:20], while James notes: "You believe that God is one; you do well: the demons also believe, and shudder" [James 2:19]. Clearly therefore, the **oneness** of God is a biblical truth. The question thus is: *What does Scripture mean by one God?* In the Old Testament, the words *el, eloah,* and *elohim,* all from related roots, are generic designations of God. The New Testament term is theos. These titles, when used of the true God, simply suggest the nature or quality of being divine- deity. The word "God" is not the name of a personality; it is the name of a **nature**, a quality of being.

When it is said, therefore, that there is but one God, the meaning is: **there is but one divine nature.** There is a **unified** set of traits or characteristics that distinguish a personality as God. It is also clear that the Scriptures teach that there is a personal distinction between those individuals identified in the New Testament as the Father, the Son, and the Holy Spirit, and these personalities are in some sense **three.**

Furthermore, additional biblical data reveal that each of these three persons is God—i.e. each possesses the quality or nature of **divinity**. The Father is divine [Ephesians 1:3], as also the Son is [Hebrews 1:8], and the Holy Spirit [Acts 5:3-4]. Any elementary student of logic knows perfectly well that the Godhead cannot be both one and three without a logical contradiction being involved—if the adjectives "one" and "three" are employed **in the identical sense.**

The fact of the matter is, they are not used in the same sense. There is but **one** divine **nature,** but there are **three** distinct **personalities** possessing that unified set of infinite qualities. Thus, there is no contradiction at all.

The work and office of the Holy Spirit transcends everything that man has ever known about God. If we miss the Holy

Spirit we would have missed the Father and Jesus. God could not commence the process of creation in the absence of the Holy Spirit. Benny Hinn, in his book "*Good morning Holy Spirit,*" describes Him as the power behind creation. When God speaks the Holy Spirit is called to action.

The earth was formless and void or a waste and emptiness, and darkness was upon the face of the deep [primeval ocean that covered the unformed earth]. **The Spirit of God** *was moving (hovering, brooding) over the face of the waters.* Genesis 1:2 (AMP)

It thus appears that without the Holy Spirit the spoken word loses potency, strength and direction. Why the Holy Spirit? Without the Holy Spirit the birth and conception of

Jesus would be impossible. The birth of Jesus defied the normal biological process of birth. Mary knew no man and her inquisitive mind asked, "How can this be, since l do know no man" The response of the angel was **"The Holy Spirit** will come upon you and the power of the Highest will overshadow you" [Luke 1:34-35]. He is the power behind Jesus's ministry. Before Jesus was ushered into ministry the Holy Spirit descended and shone upon Him during His baptism. He sustained the temptation of the devil through the Holy Spirit. You can never escape or conquer temptation without the Holy Spirit. Whenever we lead ourselves into temptation it results in sin. The bible says, "Then Jesus was led by the **[Holy] Spirit** into the wilderness **to be tempted** by the devil" [Matthew 4:1].

The Holy Spirit is the source of the anointing. The evidence of the anointing is healing, preaching, deliverance and miracles amongst the several manifestations.

The Spirit of the Lord God is upon me, because the Lord has anointed and commissioned me. To bring good news to the humble and afflicted; He has sent me to bind up [the wounds of] the brokenhearted, to proclaim release [from confinement and condemnation] to the [physical and spiritual] captives and freedom to prisoners. Isaiah 61:1 (AMP)

So, He anointed Jesus Christ to perform and He went about doing good. As detailed in the book of Acts:

How God anointed Jesus of Nazareth with the Holy Spirit and with great power; and He went around doing good and healing all who were oppressed by the devil, because God was with Him. Acts 10:3 (AMP)

He is the source of life, for the Spirit does not die. Jesus died a gruesome death when He handed over His Spirit to the Father; otherwise He would not have died. Once you put the Holy Spirit into a body it comes into life. He is the power behind resurrection. He raised Jesus Christ from the dead. The Apostle Paul says:

And if the Spirit of Him who raised Jesus from the dead lives in you, He who raised Christ Jesus from the dead will also give life to your mortal bodies through His Spirit, who lives in you. Romans 8:11 (AMP)

He is the custodian of the truth. His sentimental value is that He guides the church in truth. Ananias and Sapphira are evidence of this quality. They tried to lie to Him but to no avail. The bible says:

However, when He, the Spirit of truth, has come, He will guide you into all truth; for He will not speak on His own authority, but whatever He hears He will speak; and He will tell you things to come. John 16:13 (NKJV)

We cannot become what God wants us to be or be effective witnesses of Jesus Christ without the Holy Spirit. The Holy Spirit is a partner just as a wife is to her husband or as a corporate partner, and sister nations or sister organizations are to each other. That is the role of the Holy Spirit. He comes in to be loved, cherished and to empower and bless you in return. There is nothing in this world that can be compared to having a steadfast relationship with him, for He is a person. You greet Him, acknowledge His presence, and honor him. If you must be an expert then become an expert in entertaining Him, and once you get hold of Him, don't let Him go.

There is no logical reason how Moses was able to live in the Midian desert for 40 years [Acts 7:30]. The hostility of the environment could have been an incentive enough to prompt him to go back to Egypt, yet he did not. The purpose of the Holy Spirit in our lives is to help us. In the gospel of John, Christ says:

But the Helper, the Holy Spirit, whom the Father will send in My name, He will teach you all things, and bring to your remembrance all things that I said to you. John 14:26 (NKJV)

There is absolutely nothing that pleases the Holy Spirit than your obedience. As the Israelites journeyed through the desert they set camp at Kadesh confronted by the problem of the absence of water. They began to murmur and complain to Moses saying "Why did you bring us up out of Egypt to this terrible place? It has no grain or figs, grapevines or pomegranates. **And there is no water to drink!"** [Numbers 20:5]. Moses inquired from the Lord and he was instructed to **speak to the rock** and water would gush out. As result of anger Moses stroke the rock twice instead of speaking to it. The Lord response was "Because you have not believed (trusted) Me, to treat Me as holy in the sight of the sons of Israel, you therefore **shall not** bring this assembly into

the land which I have given them".

When the children of Israel saw the water gushing out of the rock they were euphoric and some probably marveled at the caliber of Man of God Moses was. He seemed to be a miracle wagon shape-shifting within the dimensions of wonders. When the people reignited their thought pattern from the 10 (ten) plagues in Egypt, parting the Red Sea, glowing with glory to ultimately the water miracle they just marveled. Little did the people know that the water they were drinking was a result of disobedience.

Results are not a guarantee or a sign that you were obedient to the Holy Spirt. The children of Israel still drank the water, you can still get married, you can still get to university name it. It's only the arrival at your destiny that shows that you were obedient to the Holy Spirt. When others were crossing into the promised land Moses could only stand and watch from the rock on that day it was clear disobedience cost him his destiny. Results are not a guarantee nor a sign of your obedience to the Holy ghost its only reaching your destiny that shows your obedience.

Without the Help of the Holy Spirit, Moses could have possibly died in the desert. Even demons do not break into people's lives, but enter through open doors which we open by our mouths or our actions. The Holy Spirit is like a gentleman, and only comes to a place where He is invited to. Moses perfected his relationship with the Holy Ghost in the desert. He sought Him, and the Spirit sustained him in the midst of loneliness, guilt, fear and drastic conditions. We need the Holy Ghost, to be desperate for Him to fill us again.

Chapter 5

His Voice and His manifestations

If you can't respond to the manifestations of God, you can't respond to his voice.

*And **when forty years had passed**, an Angel of the Lord appeared to him in a flame of fire in a bush, in the wilderness of Mount Sinai. When Moses saw it, he marveled at the sight; and as he drew near to observe, the voice of the Lord came to him, saying, 'I am the God of your fathers—the God of Abraham, the God of Isaac, and the God of Jacob.' And Moses trembled and dared not look.*
Acts 7:30-32 (NKJV)

After the completion of 40 years God spoke to Moses. Every divine call has a considerable time of preparation. There is no plane that takes flight before it races on the run-way. God does not entrust people with his work that are ill prepared. At the center of God's heart are his people. The currency of God is His people. A doctor goes through several years of preparation to handle patients, how much more is required to handle the work of God. The basis of the matter is, if you abscond your preparation class, you will delay your call flight.

The scenery of a burning bush in a desert was a sight to behold in an area of scarce vegetation. This stirred the imagination of Moses and he **drew near** to see. If Moses had passed on he would have missed the encounter with God. **If you can't respond to the manifestations of God, you can't respond to his voice.**

The voice of God is everything when you capture it, but it is not found in everything. There are several voices that compete for our ears. When the prophet Elijah encountered God in 1 Kings 19:11-13. Initially there was a great strong wind. The wind was so enormous that it tore the mountain. Its typical of God even Psalmist says "The earth sees and trembles, mountains melt like wax before him" [Psalm 97:4-7 (NKJV)]. At Pentecost He came like a mighty rushing wind. Irrespective of these vast indicators God was not in the wind. What followed was an earthquake. When God released Paul and Silas from prison, He used an earthquake as a medium of change the Book of Acts says, "and there was a great earthquake and the foundations of the prison shook". Even though God can use earthquakes in the encounter with the prophet Elijah the bible says "But God was not in it". What then followed was the fire. He manifested and descended at Pentecost as tongues of fire, spoke to Moses through the burning bush, accompanied Daniel, Misheck, Shadreck and Abednico in the fire, yet He was not there in the fire. After the fire was a still small voice. So it was, when Elijah heard *it*, he wrapped his face in his mantle and went out and stood in the entrance of the cave. Suddenly a voice *came* to him, and said, "What are you doing here, Elijah?" [1 Kings 19:13]

The most important question would be **How to hear God's voice. Does God speak to everyone? In which ways does he speak?**

Samuel could hear God but could not perceive that it was God speaking. This is one of the greatest pandemonium most Christians face. We have preconceived ideas on how God should speak. In the pond of our misconceptions we miss the voice of God. God cannot be compartmentalized to speak in one way. He is far bigger than what our minds can comprehend the prophet Isaiah says:

"For as the heavens are higher than the earth, So are My ways higher than your ways, And My thoughts than your thoughts. Isaiah 55:9 (NKJV)

The first step to hear God is to cast away any preconception on How God speaks. Hearing God is not an achievement. The king Abimelech by pursuing Abrahams wife encountered God in the dream [Genesis 20:3]. The king of Babylon Belshazzar by using the vessels that were reserved for the Lords temple, saw the hand of God [Daniel 5: 24-25]. In this note it's not your righteousness that positions you to hear

God. **God speaks to you according to his purpose not your conduct.** It's not something to brag about. God is more willing to speak to us than how we can comprehend his voice. In the book of Job, he says he speaks in different ways and when not heard in one way he chooses another:

"For God speaks once, and even twice, yet no one notices it [including you, Job]. "In a dream, a vision of the night [one may hear God's voice], when deep sleep falls on men while slumbering upon the bed. Job 33:14-15 (AMP)

God has promised to lead His children by His Spirit and enable them to know His voice. That means you can learn to know exactly what the Spirit of God is saying to you about **every situation.** You don't have to go through life blindly making decisions or relying on your own abilities.

When you learn to tune in to God's voice, it won't be an occasional event but an everyday part of life. That's why, in the New Testament in Mathew 13:9 (NKJV) Jesus said, "He who has ears to hear, let him hear,". There can never be a predefined formula to hear Him as He works out his ways differently in our lives. However, will present diagnostic points that will help in this venture as adapted from Kenneth Copeland:

1. Check Your Receiver

Then [with a deep longing] you will seek Me and require Me [as a vital necessity] and [you will] find Me when you search for Me with all your heart. Jeremiah 29:13 (AMP)

Have you ever tried to watch television or listen to the radio without turning it on? Of course not! You already know that if you don't turn on the receiver, you're not going to hear a thing. When you do turn them on, you fully expect to hear something! So, how do you check your spiritual receiver? The one way to know if your spiritual receiver is turned on is to answer this question:

Do you expect to hear from God?

Some people say, *Well, God just doesn't talk to me.* But, here is an important truth: even if you don't feel like God speaks to you—He does. In fact, He's speaking to you right now. But, if you aren't expecting to hear from Him, you haven't even turned on the receiver!

Now, let's be clear—He isn't going to scream, yell and demand that you pay attention. He is always speaking to you, but He speaks in "a still small voice" [1 Kings 19:12, NKJV]. So to hear Him, you have to tune in and listen carefully. Another way to describe the way we hear God's voice is through an *inward witness*.

What is an inward witness?

God doesn't communicate with us the way we communicate with one another. He communicates from His Spirit to your spirit, and then your spirit communicates what you hear to your mind. That is what we call an inward witness. It is very similar to a thought or a prompting. It's very subtle and requires a closeness with God and **regular practice to hear it more quickly and clearly.**

That's why the more time you spend with the Lord and the more you practice tuning in to His voice, the more it will become a voice that "thunders in marvelous ways" [Job 37:5, NIV].

How do you come to a place where you know whether it's you or the Lord?

Certainty in knowing that you are hearing God's voice comes to the person who is united with Him [1 Corinthians 6:17, NIV]. United means "joined," or "in union." It doesn't apply to someone who is not living for God. It applies to whomever seeks him diligently, spends time fellowshipping with Him through prayer, and obeys the commands in His Word. A receiver who is intact and ready to tune in to the voice of God is one who is expecting to hear from him, and is willing to learn to know His voice.

2. Find His Frequency

"They know his voice" –John 10:4 (NKJV)

There was once a time when you had to work to tune in to a program on the radio or television set. You had to find the right frequency. You never questioned if it was broadcasting—you knew it was—but you had to do your part to find the frequency and tune in.

How do you locate the frequency God uses to speak to you?

Most often, we miss His frequency because we're tuned in to hear some huge revelation; when, in fact, He is giving simple instructions. That's what He will do when you first begin to hear from Him—and He will continue to do this for the rest of your life here on earth. Obedience in the simple things is very important to God—it reveals the willingness of you heart.

So, if you're waiting for God to send you out to part the Red Sea, you may be missing what He's saying to you right now—which might be to clean out your closet or stop watching certain television shows or spend more time with your children. He will talk to you about the small things in your life that you need to change—adjustments you need to make. He will begin to deal with you where you are, which most often involves helping you walk in God's best by getting rid of things that are holding you back.

God wants liberty and freedom for our lives, and that begins with training. He teaches us how to be led by the Spirit. But, if we disobey these promptings in the little things, we won't graduate to the bigger assignments. Sometimes, the small things He asks of us may seem unimportant or involve giving up things we think we enjoy. But to reach a level of intimacy with God where we hear His voice and were he has launched us into new places in the spirit, obedience must become a non-negotiable factor in our lives. That's why Matthew 18 tells us to become like little children—which means not to be high-minded and think we're all-knowing. To find God's frequency, you must be willing to hear His voice in the small things.

3. Learn to Discern His Voice

"My sheep hear my voice."—John 10:27 (KJV)

If your spouse or closest friend calls you on the telephone, do you know it's them before they tell you? Most likely you do! But how? Because you've spent so much time with them, the sound of their voice and their way of saying things has become well-known to you—easy to recognize. The same is true when it comes to our relationship with God.

If you want to get to a place where you don't have to wonder whose voice you're hearing—yours, the devil's or God's—you need to spend time with the Lord. A lot of time. But, if you keep your mind and your heart full of the things of this world, it will be difficult for you to differentiate between the Spirit of God and your own thoughts. That is the definition of a carnal mind—one that has not been renewed by the Word of God.

The more time you spend with Him, the more certain you'll become about hearing God's voice. It isn't just time talking to Him, though. We learn His voice when we listen to His voice. That's why in Matthew 17:5 He said, "This is My beloved Son…listen to Him!"

4. Line It Up With His Word—the Bible

"All Scripture is inspired by God." –2 Timothy 3:16 (NASB)

One sure way to know if you're hearing God's voice is to line up what you hear against the Word of God. God will never tell you to do, think or say anything contrary to His Word. If you have a thought and you don't know if it's God or not—you can look it up in the Bible and settle it right away.

The Spirit of God will only tell you to do things that will give you a more abundant life. Every change He tells you to make is designed to bring blessing into your life and minister grace to you. So, He isn't going to tell you to refuse to forgive someone or spend money frivolously, or anything else that doesn't match His Word.

God always agrees with His written Word, and His Word always agrees with Him. In fact, Psalm 138:2 (NKJV) says He has magnified His Word even above His Name. That means God has put His Name on His written Word the way we would put our name at the bottom of a contract. He has given us His Word as a covenant and signed it in the Name of Jesus, by the blood of Jesus. Since God cannot lie, there is no way He will ever do or say anything contrary to that Word. He has absolutely joined Himself to it forever.

God trains us to recognize His voice through His written Word. He uses it to tune our spiritual ears to what is real so that we can easily recognize a counterfeit. When you're trained to hear God's voice in His Word, the devil won't be able to sneak deceptions in on you. When he tries to razzle-dazzle you with some religious-sounding voice that says, "I love you, my son. But it's just not my will to heal you at this time," you won't buy it. You'll rise up and say, "That's not the voice of God. That's a lie from hell because it doesn't agree with the Word that says, 'By His stripes we are healed'" [Isaiah 53:5, NKJV].

To live in confidence that you are hearing from Him, you need to have a knowledge of His Word continually in your heart. And you do this by drawing near to God [James 4:8]. That's your part—to seek Him. God's not going to run you down. Your part is to diligently seek Him. That involves spending time in the Word and in prayer. And whatever place you give Him in your life, the Spirit of God will fill it up for you.

The best part about hearing God's voice?

You won't just avoid counterfeit voices—you'll be given access to secrets and revelation knowledge that will make you the head and not the tail [Deuteronomy 28:13]. In Jeremiah 33:3, He says, "Call to Me and I will answer you, and I will tell you great and mighty things, which you do not know" (NASB). All you have to do is pursue a life in which you hear the voice of God, heed it and walk into a victory you never thought possible.

When you check your receiver, find His frequency, learn to discern His voice, and line up what you hear with His Word—hearing God's voice won't be an occasional event, but a lifestyle. And when someone asks you, "What is the Spirit of God telling you today?" you won't hesitate for a moment. You'll know exactly what to say.

Chapter 6

Your problem is your solution

The 40 years Moses spent in the desert were equal to the number of years he led the children of Israel in the wilderness. Your time of preparation will determine your time of service.

The people of Nineveh stood on the fringes of the beach where Jonah was spit by the fish. They had their hands clutched to their necks mired in ululation, ecstasy and utter joy. Whispers floated in the air as many waited for the sent servant to speak. You could hear many exclaim **"Our God has remembered Us"**. Nineveh was an ancient Assyrian city of Upper Mesopotamia, located on the outskirts of Mosul in modern-day northern Iraq. It is located on the eastern bank of the Tigris River, and was the capital of the Neo-Assyrian Empire. The roots of the name Nineveh simply intended **"Place of Fish"** with the goddess associated with fish or the Tigris. The act of the fish spitting Jonah was met with jubilation as it was attributed to their god, the **"god of the Sea"**.

Whilst excitement punctuated the atmosphere thoughts of bewilderment, confusion, guilt swirled like a yoyo around the mind of Jonah. The mere thought of being in the belly of the fish 3 days and 3 nights sent chills down the spine. Gastric juices, digestive enzymes enveloped Jonah's skin leaving pale patches and shadows resembling a camouflage.

In the time of its temporal prosperity Nineveh was a center of crime and wickedness characterized as "the bloody city, full of lies and robbery." In figurative language the prophet Nahum compared the Ninevites to a cruel, ravenous lion. "Upon whom," he inquired, "hath not thy wickedness passed continually?" [Nahum 3:1, 19].

Yet Nineveh, wicked though it had become, was not wholly given over to evil. He who "behold all the sons of men" [Psalm 33:13] and "seeth every precious thing" [Job 28:10] perceived in that city many who were reaching out after something better and higher, and who, if granted opportunity to learn of the living God, would put away their evil deeds and worship Him. And so, in His wisdom God revealed Himself to them in an unmistakable manner, to lead them, if possible, to repentance. The instrument chosen for this work was the prophet Jonah, the son of Amittai. To him came the word of the Lord, "Arise, go to Nineveh, that great city, and cry against it; for their wickedness is come up before Me." Jonah 1:1,2. (NKJV)

As the prophet thought of the difficulties and seeming impossibilities of this commission, he was tempted to question the wisdom of the call. From a human viewpoint it seemed as if nothing could be gained by proclaiming such a message in that proud city. He forgot for the moment that the God whom he served was all-wise and all-powerful. While he hesitated, still doubting, Satan overwhelmed him with discouragement. The prophet was seized with a great dread, and he "rose up to flee unto Tarshish." Going to Joppa, and finding there a ship ready to sail, "he paid the fare thereof and went down into it, to go with them."

If, when the call first came to him, Jonah had stopped to consider calmly, he might have known how foolish would be any effort on his part to escape the responsibility placed upon him. But not for long was he permitted to go on undisturbed in his mad flight. "The Lord sent out a great wind into the sea, and there was a might tempest in the sea, so that the ship was like to be broken. Then the mariners were afraid, and cried every man unto his god, and cast forth the wares that were in the ship into the sea, to lighten it of them. But Jonah was gone down into the sides of the ship; and he lay, and was fast asleep."

In utter amazement was the captain of the ship to find Jonah asleep as the rest of the crew and passengers were battling for their lives. They resorted to casting lots to find the culprit and the lot fell upon Jonah. "Nevertheless, the men rowed hard to bring it to the land; but they could not: for the sea wrought and was tempestuous against them. Wherefore they cried unto the Lord, and said, We beseech Thee, O Lord, we beseech Thee, let us not perish for this man's life, and lay not upon us innocent blood: for Thou, O Lord, hast done as it pleased Thee.

So they took up Jonah, and cast him forth into the sea: and the sea ceased from her raging. Then the men feared the Lord exceedingly, and offered a sacrifice unto the Lord, and made vows. **Whenever you finance disobedience you will meet storms on your way.**

At last Jonah had learned that "salvation belongeth unto the Lord." [Psalm 3:8]. With penitence and a recognition of the saving grace of God, came deliverance. Jonah was released from the perils of the mighty deep and was cast upon the dry land.

As Jonah entered the city, he began at once to "cry against", the message was, "Yet forty days, and Nineveh shall be overthrown." Jonah 3: 4(KJV). From street to street he went, sounding the note of warning. The message was not in vain. The cry that rang through the streets of the godless city was passed from lip to lip until all the inhabitants had heard the startling announcement. The Spirit of God pressed the message home to every heart and caused multitudes to tremble because of their sins and to repent in deep humbleness.

"The people of Nineveh believed God, and proclaimed a fast, and put on sackcloth, from the greatest of them even to the least of them. For word came unto the king of Nineveh, and he arose from his throne, and he laid his robe from him, and covered him with sackcloth, and sat in ashes. And he causeth it to be proclaimed and published through Nineveh by the decree of the king and his nobles, saying, Let neither man nor beast, herd nor flock, taste anything: let them not feed, nor drink water: but let man and beast be covered with sackcloth, and cry mightily unto God: yea, let them turn everyone from his evil way, and from the violence that is in their hands. Who can tell if God will turn and repent, and turn away from His fierce anger, that we perish not?". Jonah 3:5-9(NKJV) What started as an act of disobedience ended in repentance of the whole city.

Pharaoh's Dream

*Now it happened at the end of two full years that Pharaoh dreamed that he was standing by the [a]Nile. And lo, there came up out of the Nile seven [healthy] cows, sleek and handsome and fat; and they grazed in the reed grass [in a marshy pasture]. Then behold, **seven** other cows came up after them out of the Nile, ugly and gaunt and* *raw-boned, and stood by the fat cows on the bank of the Nile. Then the ugly and gaunt and raw-boned cows ate up the seven sleek and fat cows. Then Pharaoh awoke. Then he fell asleep and dreamed a second time; and behold, **seven** ears of grain came up on a single stalk, plump and good. Then behold, **seven** ears [of grain], thin and dried up by the east wind, sprouted after them. Then the thin ears swallowed the seven plump and full ears. And Pharaoh awoke, and it was a dream. Genesis 41:1-7 (AMP)*

Several years before the Joseph the dreamer was born a tale is told of the breach of contract that transpired between his father Jacob and Laban. After **seven** years of serving Laban the day of payment arrived.

As in accordance with their initial agreement Rachel the "beautiful one" would be given to Jacob as a wife. A stroke of brilliance or mere "con-artistry" in the encapsulation of the night saw Jacobs joy short lived, as the sun arose cocooned to his bed was Leah, "the cross-eyed one" not Rachel. Sadness overshadowed Jacob tears trickled from his eyes. Leah's heart leapt for joy as she was highly regarded as the uglier one. Rachel was shrouded in the mist of confusion and disappointment. The expectation of marriage was extinguished. The hallucinations and dreams of a honey moon with Jacob the "hubby" were now a nightmare. Jacob through his resilience went on to serve another **seven** years for Rachel.

Whilst some could have chosen to study medicine in the same length of time, Jacobs pursuit finally yielded as he was given his first love Rachel. She was the admiration of his eyes, the famed hard target which featured his father starring the main actor role in the "hard to get" finale, finally paid off.

Now, a bit of numerology not a big word other than the study of the significance of numbers. When Jacobs son Joseph interpreted Pharaoh's dream his interpretation was:

*Then Joseph said to Pharaoh, "The [two] dreams are one [and the same and have one interpretation]; God has shown Pharaoh what He is about to do. The **seven** good cows are **seven** years, and the **seven** good ears are seven years. The **seven** thin and ugly cows that came up after them are seven years; and also the seven thin ears, dried* *up and scorched by the east wind, they are seven years of famine and hunger. This is the message just as I have told Pharaoh: God has shown Pharaoh what He is about to do. Listen very carefully:* **seven** *years of great abundance will come throughout all the land of Egypt. Genesis 41:25-29 (AMP)*

Pharaoh's dream interpretation was basically **seven years of drought and seven years of harvest** (abundance). Could it be a mere coincidence that the father Jacob worked for **seven years for Leah** the wrong wife and the **same number of years for the right one** Rachel. **What was a problem to Jacob was a solution to Joseph.** There are problems in our history that are solutions to our future. God did not promise us that all things will feel good but they will definitely work for good [Romans 8:28].

For the Israelites walked forty years in the wilderness, until all the nation, that is, the men of war who came out of Egypt, died because they did not listen to the voice of the Lord; to them the Lord had sworn [an oath] that He would not let them see the land which He had promised to their fathers to give us, a land [of abundance] flowing with milk and honey.
Joshua 5:6 (AMP)

Moses was a shepherd, in the Midian desert, for 40 years. He went from being the prince of Egypt and a revolutionary with a dream to a nobody. But here's what's encouraging to me. During those 40 years, I'm sure Moses had a lot of questions. He had a lot of doubts. He had a lot of humility thrust upon him. And while he may have felt like he was doing nothing with his life, God was busy. And I believe God was busy in at least two ways – one outside, and one inside.

In the outside, God was busy preparing Moses to know what life was like in the desert, which would come in pretty handy when he spent the NEXT 40 years of life wandering around there. The stuff he learned about finding water, sleeping arrangements, wildlife, plant life – you name it – would be invaluable. Moses had no clue he was learning all this, but he was.

On the inside, God was also busy. He was busy helping Moses become the sort of person would could walk into the court of the most powerful man in the known world and say "Let my people go." He was preparing him to be the kind of person who could deal with the impatience and bellyaching of a newly liberated people. He was preparing him to be someone who knew what it was like to depend on the work of God and walk deeply with Him. And Moses didn't even know it. He was being prepared for something better in the desert, and he thought he was just herding sheep.

The number "40" holds sentimental value in the bible. 40 represents the end of a time of testing. Israel was in the wilderness for 40 years and so was Jesus tempted and tried of the devil for 40 days in the Judean desert. It is no accident that in the story of Noah, the rain poured for 40 days, and submerged the world in water. Just as a person leaves a **mikveh** "a Judaism bath" pure, so too when the waters of the flood subsided, the world was purified from the licentiousness which had corrupted it in the days of Noah.

Spies were sent by Moses to explore the promised land Canaan for forty days [Numbers 13:2, 25]. Moses was on Mt. Sinai for 40 days and came down with the stone tablets. The Jews arrived at Mt. Sinai as a nation of Egyptian slaves, but after 40 days they were transformed into God's nation.40 years represents the number of years it takes a generation to arise. Several Jewish leaders and kings ruled for "forty years", that is, a generation i.e. Eli [1 Samuel 4:18], Saul [Acts 13:21], David [2 Samuel 5:4], and Solomon [1 Kings 11:42].

Goliath challenged the Israelites twice a day for forty days before David defeated him [1 Samuel 17:16]. The prophet Elijah had to walk 40 days and 40 nights before arriving to mount Horeb [1 Kings 19:8]. Forty days was the period from the resurrection of Jesus to the ascension of Jesus [Acts 1:3]. According to Stephen, Moses' life is divided into three 40-year segments, separated by his growing to adulthood, fleeing from Egypt, and his return to lead his people out [Acts 7:23,30,36]. According to the Talmud, it also takes 40 days for an embryo to be formed in its mother's womb.

Every divine call attracts difficulties, tests and troubles. If you are called to serve Him you will definitely encounter difficulties to prepare you for the future endeavours. The troubles the pains you go through are not necessarily there to kill you, they are solutions to the people you will minister to. So, God is busy loading solutions for his people in you, yeah through the troubles you encounter. **There is nothing you have been through that will be put to waste.** That pain will come for good one day. The 40 years Moses spent in the desert were equal to the number of years he led the children of Israel in the wilderness. Your time of preparation will determine your time of service. Your problem is not necessarily an obstacle, **your problem is your solution.**

Chapter 7

Receiving the Art

You need the Light. Jacob had to endure another seven years of labour because he married in the night. There can never be real sight in the absence of light.

*Regarding this **salvation**, the prophets who prophesied about the grace [of God] that was intended for you, searched carefully and inquired [about this future way of salvation], seeking to find out what person or what time the Spirit of Christ within them was indicating as He foretold the sufferings of Christ and the glories [destined] to follow. It was revealed to them that their services [their prophecies regarding grace] were not [meant] for themselves and their time, but for you, in these things [the death, resurrection, and glorification of Jesus Christ] which have now been told to you by those who preached the gospel to you by the [power of the] Holy Spirit [who was] sent* *from heaven.* **Into these things even the angels long to look.** *1 Peter 1:10-12 (AMP)*

Our focus beams into the last words of the extracted text **"Into these things even the angels long to".** Which things are these?

These are the things contained in the salvation package. Of all the messages angels wish they knew the message of salvation. There are two different Greek words that describe the phrase **"to look".** One means to stand on tiptoe, as if you are at the back of a crowd trying to watch a parade. The other means to stoop down. It's the same word used for Peter and John stooping to look inside the empty tomb on Easter Sunday morning. The angels are so eager to understand God's grace that they stand on tiptoe and bend down from the battlements of heaven to marvel at the unfolding plan of salvation. This is exactly the reverse of the way we think of it. If I told you that I had a special door that lets you look into the realm of the angels, all of you would crowd around to get a glimpse of "the other side." But the Bible never encourages us to peek into the angelic realm. Here we are told the angels long to look at and understand our salvation.

Why would the angels marvel at our salvation? The answer is clear. There are no "saved" angels because salvation is not for them, but for us. Jesus died to redeem fallen men and women, not the angels. There are elect and non-elect angels; there are good angels and bad angels; there are obedient and disobedient angels, but there are no "saved" angels. Only humans can be saved. Only humans can be redeemed. We alone of all the creatures in the universe can experience the wonders of God's saving grace. This fascinates the angels, and causes them to study and ponder the mysteries of a salvation they do not share.

Here is Peter's message made plain: God loves you so much, the angels are amazed. They know nothing about grace and mercy and forgiveness. They've never experienced new life, the new birth, regeneration, the indwelling of the Holy Spirit, or the wonder of deliverance from sin. That which we have experienced in Jesus Christ, the angels never knew and will never know. We are far more privileged than they.

Here is our greatest sin—taking for granted what God has done for us. Those things that cause the angels to rejoice (even one sinner who comes to repentance—Luke 15:10), makes us bored stiff. But when you are bored with God, even heaven doesn't have a better alternative.

By redemption we qualify for the riches in Christ. Salvation places all believers at an equal opportunity to receive all what Christ died for. God's mode of giving is by inheritance. The Apostle Paul says in the book of Romans:

And if [we are His] children, [then we are His] heirs also: heirs of God and fellow heirs with Christ [sharing His spiritual blessing and inheritance], if indeed we share in His suffering so that we may also share in His glory. Romans 8:17 (AMP)

By adoption, sonship we are joint heirs with Christ. What it essentially means is that we share in glory what Christ died for. The bible says for the joy that was set before him he endured death by the cross [Hebrews 12:2]. In the book of revelation 5:12 we are given a list of the rewards that were given to Christ. **Obedience is always rewarded.** By merit of dying at the cross for the redemption of man-kind Christ received power, riches, wisdom, strength, honour, glory, and blessing. The seven things that Christ died for constitute what we earlier on referred to as the "salvation package".

Saying with a loud voice, Worthy is the Lamb that was slain to receive power, and riches, and wisdom, and strength, and honour, and glory, and blessing. Revelation 5:12 (KJV)

The striking sight is, how come we find some Christians in their current plight if we have all have access the riches in Christ at our disposal. How come the lives of some, perhaps most Christians seem to live a life not reflective of what Christ died for. My spiritual father in the same context asserts that some Christians tend to live a life as if they found the cross crowded, found the blood of Christ clotted. It's as if the blood of Christ is no longer as powerful today as it was ago. It still holds the same redemptive, cleansing and sanctification power today:

How much more shall the blood of Christ, who through the eternal Spirit offered himself without spot to God, purge your conscience from dead works to serve the living God? Hebrews 9:14 (KJV)

What then can be our conclusion? There is nothing wrong with God, he has already provided everything pertaining to life and godliness [Ephesians 1:3]. God has already given; the problem lies with us we have **failed to receive**. Receiving goes beyond qualifying to be granted it's a deliberate strategy to guarantee what has been provided. Rightfully stated receiving is not just a mere stance it's an art. Whilst the church over emphasizes giving there should be an intentional posture to teach how to receive.

To be able to receive there are essential ingredients that are required. At the center Of God's agenda with man is the Holy Spirit. If we fail to receive Him, we fail as well to receive all that He carries. How do you think the Holy Spirit feels when people are busy asking for his gifts not Himself? I would rather pray for him to continually fill me, l get Him, l get His gifts as well.

*And I will pray the Father, and he shall give you another Comforter, that he may abide with you for ever; Even the Spirit of truth; whom the world **cannot receive**, because it **seeth** him not, neither **knoweth** him: but ye know him; for he dwelleth with you, and shall be in you. John 14:16-17 (KJV)*

Paying attention to the text we realise that they failed to **receive Him** for two basic reasons: their inability to see and know. When God spoke to his servant Abraham "the father of many nations" we established that the inheritance of the nations was going to be determined by just one sense, sight [Genesis 13:15]. Sight is a light issue. How illuminated you are by his word, determines your capacity to receive. The Psalmist David writes, "thy word is a lamp unto my feet and a **light** unto my path" [Psalm 119:105].

There is nothing we can receive in the Kingdom of God unless it is illuminated by his word. The word determines how far we can cast our eyes of faith. God in his conversation with Abraham he said "As far as your eyes can see. I will give you the nations as your inheritance" [Genesis 13:15]. The parable of the lost coin is another demonstration of the dependency of sight to light. Even God himself could not create in the absence of Light. There is nothing we can do in his kingdom in the absence of Light i.e. his word. **You need the**

Light. Jacob had to endure another seven

years of labour because he married in the night. There can never be real sight in the absence of light.

The second aspect is knowledge. We can only know we have received if its confirmed by our knowledge of it. Sometimes we are blind to what we have received because we don't have knowledge of it. How much you pursue your vision is simply a function of how much you know about it. How far you can go is also a function of knowledge. A car can only go as far as the amount of fuel in its tank. All professions have their foundations in several years of academic quest. The bible says my people perish cause of the lack of knowledge [Hosea 4:6]. It places death and life as a function of the abundance and scarcity of knowledge. Your knowledge deficit is the determinant of whether you are alive or simply "the walking dead". The book of Proverbs in relation to knowledge states that:

The heart of the prudent getteth knowledge; and the ear of the wise seeketh knowledge. Proverbs 18:15 (KJV)

Another essential aspect is expectation. We can never receive what we don't expect. Expectation is the mother of all manifestation. In the book of Acts a man who was lame from birth lay at the gate of the temple called Beautiful. The bible says he gave heed to Peter and John **expecting to receive from them** [Acts 3:5]. We all know how this man went on to be healed though the ministration of Peter. The key to his healing was expectation. He may have expected money, but the same seed of expectation was channeled to healing. The bible says, "the expectation of the righteous shall not be cut off" [Proverbs 23:18].

Expectation is the fertile breeding ground for miracles, signs and wonders.

Receiving is deliberate. **A closed mouth is a closed destiny.** If salvation requires a deliberate proclamation from your mouth of the Lordship of Jesus Christ. How much more then should we proclaim to receive its benefits. Life and death lie in the power of the tongue. It is the tongue that shapes the words that we speak. For every declaration that is made in God's presence receivers shout "I receive". In as much the substance is spiritual the physical actions matter. As much as the breaking of the bread, drinking of the wine and water baptism are significant physical actions they resemble greater spiritual parallels. Such important are the verbal proclamations associated with receiving. The intentional proclamation should be accompanied by faith in our heart to receive. **You are not only a giver but also a receiver.**

Chapter 8

Welcome my King

My King is a sovereign King. No means of measure can define His limitless love. No far-seeing telescope can bring into visibility the coastline of His shoreless supply. Do you know Him?

I've been fortunate to have witnessed some of the most breathtaking views on earth. From the Rocky Mountains of the African terrain, to the jungles of Belize and the deltas of Okavango, God's creation is stunning. But there is a future place—an eternal dwelling—that far exceeds anything we could ever behold or fathom. Heaven is not a mythical place. It is the holy dwelling of the Lord Most High. And although we cannot even begin to comprehend its splendor, the Bible gives us beautiful descriptions of the place in which those who have received Jesus will spend eternity.

In my Father's house are many mansions: if it were not so, I would have told you. I go to prepare a place for you. And if I go and prepare a place for you, I will come again, and receive you unto myself; that where I am, there ye may be also. John 14:2-3 (KJV)

From the apex of the city, I can see impressive-looking homes dotting the landscape of the foothills. Considered mansions by the world's standards, I know they don't even come close to the mansions prepared for the saints in heaven. Before His death, Jesus comforted the twelve with the promise that he would go and provide a place for them. The most beautiful part was His assurance that He would return for them and receive them unto Himself. No matter how spectacular the mansions in our Father's house, dwelling with Jesus will be the most beautiful habitation of all. Welcomed into heaven by the Way, the Truth, and the Life, will be the culmination of the hope we have in Christ.

We will dwell with Him as He sits upon his throne. Taking a leaf from SM Lockridge's classical sermon "That's my King":

- He is a seven-way king.
- He's the King of the Jews; that's a racial king.
- He's the King of Israel; that's a national King.
- He's the King of Righteousness.
- He's the King of the Ages.
- He's the King of Heaven.
- He's the King of Glory.
- He's the King of Kings, and He's the Lord of Lords

The Heavens declare the glory of God and the firmament shows His handiwork. My King is a sovereign King. No means of measure can define His limitless love. No far-seeing telescope can bring into visibility the coastline of His shoreless supply. No barrier can hinder Him from pouring out His blessings.

- He's enduringly strong.
- He's entirely sincere.
- He's eternally steadfast.
- He's immortally graceful.
- He's imperially powerful.
- He's impartially merciful.

Do you know Him?

- He's the greatest phenomenon that ever crossed the horizon of this world.
- He's God's Son.
- He's a sinner's Savior.
- He's the centerpiece of civilization.
- He stands in the solitude of Himself.
- He's awesome.
- He's unique.
- He's unparalleled.

- He's unprecedented.
- He's the loftiest idea in literature.
- He's the highest personality in philosophy.
- He's the supreme problem in higher criticism.
- He's the fundamental doctrine of true theology.
- He's the cardinal necessity of spiritual religion.
- He's the miracle of the age.
- He's the superlative of everything good that you choose to call Him.
- He's the only one qualified to be an all sufficient Savior

I wonder if you know Him today?

- He supplies strength for the weak.
- He's available for the tempted and the tried.
- He sympathizes, and He saves.

- He strengthens and sustains.
- He guards, and He guides.
- He heals the sick.
- He cleanses lepers.
- He forgives sinners.
- He discharges debtors.
- He delivers captives.
- He defends the feeble.
- He blesses the young.
- He serves the unfortunate.
- He regards the aged.
- He rewards the diligent.
- And He beautifies the meek.

I wonder if you know Him? Well, my King is *the* King.

- He's the key to knowledge.
- He's the wellspring to wisdom.
- He's the doorway of deliverance.
- He's the pathway of peace.

- He's the roadway of righteousness.
- He's the highway of holiness.
- He's the gateway of glory

Do you know Him? Well.

- His office is manifold.
- His promise is sure.
- His light is matchless.
- His goodness is limitless.
- His mercy is everlasting.
- His love never changes.
- His Word is enough.
- His grace is sufficient.
- His reign is righteous.
- And His yoke is easy, and his burden is light.

I wish I could describe Him to you, but

- He's indescribable.
- He's incomprehensible.

- He's invincible.
- He's irresistible.

Well,

- You can't get Him out of your mind.
- You can't get Him off your hand.
- You can't out live Him,
- And you can't live without Him.
- The Pharisees couldn't stand Him, but they found out they couldn't stop Him.
- Pilate couldn't find any fault in Him.
- The witnesses couldn't get their testimonies to agree.
- Herod couldn't kill Him.
- Death couldn't handle Him,
- And the grave couldn't hold Him.

Yea! That's my King, Our heavenly father. I don't know what made you read this book or how you came to know of it, but I believe it was a Godly ordained appointment, divinely engineered. I believe in a free, jubilant, happy you, walking in the light of God's word. By the grace of God, we will meet one day in the corridors of power, maybe in the parking lots, it can be in a lift or even the staircases of heaven, only God knows. We are gifted differently, we serve different purposes in this world. I believe you have what it takes to change this world. Go out there, change lives, transform communities, shake the world. Be effective to such an extent that even when you have passed on someone somewhere will go down on his knees one day and say, "Thank you Lord for this person who once lived", and finally:

Let your light so shine before men, that they may see your good works, and glorify your Father which is in heaven. Matthew 5:16 (KJV)